THE BUILDING OF
STONEHENGE

by Morgan Beard

Running Press
Hachette Book Group
1290 Avenue of the Americas, New York, NY 10104
www.runningpress.com
@Running_Press

First Edition: July 2012

Published by Running Press, an imprint of Perseus Books, LLC,
a subsidiary of Hachette Book Group, Inc.

The Hachette Speakers Bureau provides a wide range of authors for speaking events. To find out more, go to www.hachettespeakersbureau.com or call (866) 376-6591.

The publisher is not responsible for websites (or their content) that are not owned by the publisher.

ISBN: 978-0-7624-4335-2

CONTENTS

INTRODUCTION

Everyone loves a mystery, and few mysteries have captured people's imaginations like the ruins of Stonehenge. This ancient stone arrangement rests in the Salisbury Plain in Wiltshire, Southern England, and contains over 150 rocks, some weighing forty metric tons each (or the equivalent weight of six elephants). Stonehenge is not the only "henge" in Britain. In fact, since a "henge" is a generic term for any wide, circular enclosure, there are over fifty to choose from. However,

Stonehenge is one of the largest and most complex.

For this reason, Stonehenge has fascinated visitors for over five millennia, and yet the who, how, and why remain pure speculation. Modern science has begun to shed light on these mysteries by using new technology like radiocarbon dating and computers, but most of Stonehenge's secrets remain as illusive and intriguing as ever.

THE BUILDERS

Over the years, a variety of people, cultures, and species have been given credit for the building of Stonehenge. Some of the most legendary figures trying to take responsibility have included:

Giants: According to old myths, dancing giants were caught in a sunbeam and petrified to stone, causing the monument to be nicknamed the "Giant's Ring." The stones were also believed to have healing power.

Merlin and King Arthur: Some believe that Merlin himself assembled Stonehenge to commemorate slain chieftains. It's also rumored that the Sword in the Stone, which would eventually lead Arthur onto the throne and into legend, was made from Stonehenge stones.

Aliens: Most of the world's earliest and most elaborate crop circles are found within a forty-mile (64 km) radius of Stonehenge. Scientists today are unable to replicate crop circles, suggesting that their construction and that of Stonehenge should perhaps be credited to a more intelligent species.

Atlanteans: According to Plato, the Kingdom of Atlantis controlled the islands of the Atlantic and built many stone structures to better predict future events based on astronomical calculations. Given the fate of Atlantis, which supposedly sank into the sea, it's debatable how accurate their predictions could have been.

Druids: John Aubrey, a Stonehenge scholar, erroneously suggested this connection three centuries ago. The Druids are an earth-based faith that we now know formed much later than the building of Stonehenge. The Druids do celebrate the summer solstice, same as Stonehenge's true builders, and they have recently made it a tradition to incorporate this ancient monument into current rituals.

It is almost easier to believe magic created Stonehenge than to acknowledge that, mind-bogglingly enough, it was probably done by societies yet to invent the wheel. Current archeological evidence suggests three societies built the monument over a two-thousand-year period. There is still contention about which people are responsible and for what, but the general consensus is that ancient Britons built the site. Trying to picture people from over five thousand years ago may conjure up images of cavemen in animal skins hunting wooly mammoths, but in reality the people of that time were not that different from you and me. They wore clothes made of leather or woven fabric, carved pins to hold their hair in place, and made jewelry with pendants and beads. They had a far-reaching trade network, were great sailors, and had begun to craft metal and stone tools.

The **Beaker Folk** from 2500 BC are believed to have done some of the work on Stonehenge. They were an aggressive culture that invaded the Salisbury Plain. From artifacts, we know that the Beakers were sophisticated, organized, understood mathematics, worshipped the sun, and celebrated the solstices. This makes them ideal builders for some of the site.

The other cultures that contributed to Stonehenge remain a mystery, though archeologists are getting closer and closer to finding answers.

CREATING
STONEHENGE

Appropriately enough, Stonehenge was started in the Stone Age. Up to three prehistoric cultures poured a combined thirty million hours of labor into the project, and the result is a stunning reminder of the creativity, intelligence, and technology possessed by our ancient ancestors. The story of how these civilizations built Stonehenge is one of persistence and, above all, patience. Stonehenge itself was built in three phases.

Phase I

Almost five thousand years ago in about 3100 BC, the first construction began. A circular ditch nearly 288 feet (87 m) in diameter was dug, and placed within it were fifty-six wooden posts. These wooden posts were inserted into **Aubrey Holes**, named after their discoverer, John Aubrey. Four **Station Stones** were also probably placed perpendicular to the midsummer sunrise during this phase, but there is debate suggesting this might have happened later on.

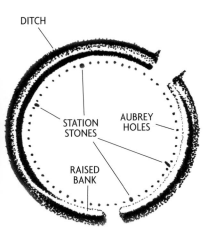

DITCH

STATION STONES

AUBREY HOLES

RAISED BANK

Phase II

The Beaker Folk are believed to have contributed to this phase. They moved a number of **bluestones**, each weighing about four metric tons, 240 miles (386 km) from rock quarries in the Preseli Mountains. These stones were transported over rivers and open-seas, and they were moved on land by pushing sledges over a series of rolling logs.

The Beakers set these bluestones in an incomplete double circle, enlarged the ditch, and added the **"Avenue"** to the site. The Avenue would eventually run nearly two miles from the River

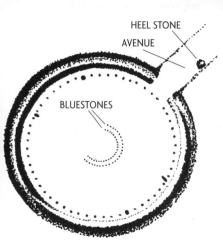

HEEL STONE

AVENUE

BLUESTONES

Avon to the northeastern entrance of Stonehenge with parallel banks. This pathway was probably a ceremonial entrance, as it is aligned with the midsummer sunrise that dawns right above it. The Beakers also placed the **Heel Stone**, weighing thirty-two metric tons, in the Avenue.

The Beaker's vision for Stonehenge was ambitious but never completed. The site was abandoned around 2500 BC.

This phase is a bit contested. Some believe the bluestones weren't moved until Phase 3 and that Phase 2 saw only the building of a timber circle.

Phase III

Around 2300 BC, Stonehenge was built into what we see today. To create this finished appearance, sarsen rock, a type of sandstone, was transported twenty miles (32 km) from Marlborough Downs using sledges and log-rollers. The rock was then fashioned with "mauls," a type of hammer, to shape the surfaces.

Thirty of these neatly trimmed stones went into the **Sarsen Circle**. Each of the thirty was about thirteen feet high (4 m), over six feet wide (2 m), and three feet thick (1 m). They were

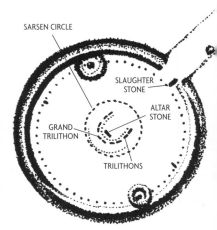

SARSEN CIRCLE

SLAUGHTER STONE

ALTAR STONE

GRAND TRILITHON

TRILITHONS

capped with lintels, or horizontal stones, that were hoisted with a complicated leverage system into the air and on top of these base stones. Hammered to curve in a circle and with joints to secure the stones, these lintels created a thirteen-foot-high (4 m) circle in the air—a height kept consistent all the way around to within a few centimeters. This precise calculation and tooling makes the Sarsen Circle the most impressive feature of Stonehenge.

The largest features of Stonehenge are the **Trilithons**, which are the largest sarsen stones forming the horse-shoe shape in the center of the Sarsen Circle. These stones weigh up to forty metric tons with the largest, the **Grand Trilithon**, up to twenty-seven feet (8 m) tall. They were erected in five pairs with five lintels to top the formation.

The **Altar Stone** and **Slaughter Stone** were also added to the structure. Despite their names, the stones were never used as altars or for slaughter. The Altar Stone lies directly in front of the Grand Trilithon, and it is the only rock made of green sandstone. The sarsen Slaughter Stone is near the northeast entrance of Stonehenge. The bluestones were also reused, set in a single ring within the Sarsen Circle and in an inner horseshoe inside the Trilithon formation.

The last modifications to Stonehenge took place between 1900 BC and 1700 BC. A series of holes, dubbed the **Y and Z holes**, were dug in concentric circles between the Sarsen Circle and the Aubrey Holes. These holes were meant to hold even more stones, but construction was halted, leaving the site abandoned once more.

To the Present Day

Stonehenge has had its share of visitors over the years, and not all of them meant well. Locals and conquerors alike dismantled and destroyed parts of the site. It wasn't until very recently, 1918 AD, that the site was transferred from private property to the British government, finally acknowledging its historical value. In 1986 AD, it was honored as a World Heritage Site and has received a wealth of support since then.

WRITTEN IN STONE

We have some information about how the stones were placed and by whom, but when it comes to why, there is very little to go on. The true meaning of Stonehenge is left mostly to our imaginations.

The most plausible explanation is that Stonehenge was used as a calendar or ancient observatory. There are several alignments between the stones and the sun and moon, including the midsummer sunrise over the Heel Stone and in between the uprights of the Grand Trilithon, a similar alignment with the midwinter sunset, and midsummer moonrise and midwinter moonset alignments with the Station Stones. From this information, the time of year could be determined, though some believe that these various rock configurations could also predict lunar and solar eclipses.

The mathematics of these alignments required the builders of Stonehenge to apply principals of the Pythagorean Theorem and pi ages before these concepts were fully discovered by the rest of the Western world. This demonstration of genius makes the possibilities for Stonehenge's true purpose nearly infinite.

While Stonehenge could easily have been an ancient observatory for the stars, there's no reason it couldn't have been a temple as well; it was often the priests' job to keep track of the stars' movements.

Of course, these potential uses for Stonehenge don't answer the question of why a temple or observatory would need to be built in the middle of Salisbury Plain, such a long distance from rock quarries. One theory that does answer this question is that of ley lines. Some suggest that the world is covered in high-energy force-fields, called ley lines, and intersections of these lines are high-power areas. Stonehenge is believed to lie on one of these intersections.

Other speculations have included everything from Stonehenge being a gateway to other worlds to the more earthly reasoning that it was used for criminal proceedings, political gatherings, or as a burial ground for high-ranking citizens.

Whatever its purpose, it's clear that the site was important to these prehistoric people, and because of the many wonders and possibilities it continues to offer us today, Stonehenge maintains its importance in the modern world.

BUILD YOUR OWN

First, take out the mat puzzle-pieces and put them together (if pieces have trouble staying together or will be in a busy area, flip pieces over, assemble puzzle upside down using back text as a guide, and tape pieces together). Next, you will see numbers on the mat; these numbers correspond to the numbers you'll find on the bottom of your stone pieces. Place your stone piece on the matching number on the mat. Arrange stones 11 and 12 with their lintels resting on the adjoining base stone. If your Stonehenge is in a busy place, a dab of glue on the stone bottoms will keep them upright.

Congratulations, you just built your own Stonehenge! Now, for an extra bit of fun, you can wait for the sunrise on the summer solstice and align your circle astronomically, just as the ancients did—Druid robes optional. Whatever purpose you ascribe to your mysterious, personal Stonehenge, may it bring you the wisdom of the ages.

This book has been bound using handcraft methods and Smyth-sewn to ensure durability.

The box was illustrated by Christopher Wormell.

The interior and site mat were illustrated by Bill Jones.

Designed by Bill Jones.

The text was written by Morgan Beard.
The text was edited by Jennifer Colella.

The text was set in Adobe Garamond and Agenda.